Listening with the heart

Listening with the heart

David Forrester

Introduction by Michael Hollings

PAULIST PRESS
New York/Ramsey/Toronto

First published in Britain, Ireland and associated territories in 1978 by Burns & Oates Ltd

Copyright © 1978 David Forrester
Introduction copyright © 1978 Michael Hollings

All rights reserved. No part of this publication may be stored in an information retrieval system, transmitted, translated or reproduced in any form or by any means whether electronic, mechanical, chemical, photocopying, recording, manuscript or otherwise, for any purpose whatsoever, in any country, without the previous written permission of Search Press Limited, 2-10 Jerdan Place, London SW6 5PT.

Acknowledgments: The author and publishers are grateful to the following for kind permission to reproduce extracts from the works cited: Darton, Longman & Todd for the *Jerusalem Bible*, Archbishop Bloom's *School for Prayer* and Simon Tugwell's *Did You Receive the Spirit?*; Wm. Collins & Sons for Martin Buber's *Between Man and God*; Sheed & Ward for Abbot John Chapman's *Spiritual Letters*, Gerald Vann's *The Heart of Man*; the SPCK for *The Way of the Pilgrim*.

ISBN: 0-8091-2183-2
Library of Congress
Catalog Card Number: 78-70822

Printed and bound in the
United States of America

Contents

		Page
	Introduction	7
	Preface	13
1	Love and prayer	15
2	Trust in God alone	25
3	Christians as seed in the earth	33
4	The value of silence and simplicity in prayer	39
5	Human growth and prayer	47
6	Prayer as a solution to loneliness	55
7	Listening with the heart in prayer	61
8	God's activity in history: the foundation of prayer	71
9	Prayer in groups: charismatic prayer	85
	Further reading	95

Introduction
by Michael Hollings

'In the beginning God created the heavens and the earth. Now the earth was a formless void, there was darkness over the deep, and God's spirit hovered over the water'. (Gen. 1:1)

This is our introduction to the beginning of things as we know them. But to read such a passage is to set up different thoughts and images. One of these for me is the sense of stillness, silence and what I would call depth. The temptation is to say that this was the atmosphere in which God dwelt before creation. But, of course, it was not an atmosphere. If I am at all right in my sensing, then what I am sensing is God.

Immediately I am brought up against a paradox which surrounds my image of God — he is ever still and ever in movement. Out of this eternal silent-still-movement who is God comes the wonder of creation, signalising to me whispering, growing and finally crashing sound in all the myriad tones and volumes which we human beings can recognise. For we too emerge at some peak of creation able to be conscious, active in body mind and heart, yet able also to be still, to listen and to appreciate the many hues and tones of God's creation. The appreciation and the listening then may and has been known to lead on beyond mere receiving to pondering whence it comes, whence we come. Men and women look for the creator, for the father-mother who begot us, and ponder the existence of God.

There is, however, always the gnawing of our stomachs. Our nature demands that we eat to survive. Food has to be found, shelter made, the species carried on by breeding, children reared.

The struggle to survive, and beyond that the natural desire to gather a little comfort round about survival, generates in each of us a certain selfishness coupled with possessiveness. This is not all bad, but has in it the germ of corruption. It seems all too easy to distract the general kind of person that we are from the one goal of developing relationships between God and ourselves, ourselves and others.

There are some ordinary people not exceptional or different from ourselves who never find themselves satisfied. The human spirit reaches out seeking tranquillity and rest, beauty and satisfaction, reaches in to the general mess which is ourselves . . . wanting, longing.

This is like a spark of negative disillusionment and positive seeking to hear God's word and do it. Most of us, but some more than others, know what it is to stand on a dark night and look at the stars, to stand in pale moonlight listening to a nightingale sing, or just to hear the contrast of natural stillness and the roar of traffic.

The very roar and noise of the modern world seem to shut us off from mystery and depth. We turn to the immediate, get caught in the rush and tumble of daily living, keeping up with each other, the cost of inflation, the drug of TV, entertainment, sport, drink and being a consumer, as well as a worker. Isn't all that God-stuff irrelevant? I have so much to do, so many worries, and

INTRODUCTION

there is never any time for things like that!

In history and even today it has been usual for men and women to go away from crowded areas to hilltops or the desert. The early Church saw the Desert Fathers flourish, St Benedict fled from Rome to the hills at Subiaco. Much later the seven founders of the Servite Order did the same thing, this time from the riches and corruption of Florence. Almost in our own day, Charles de Foucauld left society and France eventually to find his way to the Sahara.

Here there is a follower of Jesus who St Luke tells us: 'would always go off to some place where he could be alone and pray' (Lk. 5:14). For them it seems of the essence in order to obey the injunction: 'Be still and know that I am God', that they must withdraw. The proof of the authenticity of what they do in their way of life has been shown over and over again in genuine spiritual growth leading to holiness.

All this is indeed authentic, but it is only part of the world picture. Sadly, the effect of these withdrawals and the living out of a rule of life in community to some extent safeguarded from the rough and tumble of the world has been to make ordinary men and women feel holiness and indeed deeper prayer-life is reserved for monks and nuns and to a lesser degree for priests.

Faced with this problem, religious orders did two things. They opened part of their life-style by introducing laymen and women to a companionship of 'confrater' or a third order. Then newer orders like the Jesuits made the point that they were to live more in the line of the secular world. But none of this completely faced the need in the fields and on the streets and especially in the growing cities.

Outside Christianity, the reality of contemplation in

the midst of the world was stated in the Taoist classic *Saikondan:* 'The stillness in stillness is not the real stillness: only where there is stillness in movement can the spiritual rhythm appear which pervades heaven and earth'. An ancient adds: 'Meditation in activity is a thousand million times superior to meditation in repose' (*A First Zen Reader*, Trevor Leggett).

For the Christian, such thought is real in Jesus Christ, who became man and 'lived among us' (John 1:14). He was born into a world of torment and turmoil. After exile and return home as a child, he lived ordinarily in a small town among ordinary people. Later he collected friends, many of them fishermen, only a few more educated. He was surrounded by them, seldom alone, except when he escaped to pray; crowds were his way of life, which was not settled or stable, but more nomadic. If the people of Israel of Moses' day were a pilgrim people, and the Christian Church today is also on pilgrimage, Christ certainly followed the movement of the prophets and foreshadowed the need not simply to settle down which has been a characteristic temptation since the beginning.

There are still today very different ways of approaching God and growing into deeper relationship with him, stretching from the isolation of the hermit to the common-living of monks nuns or lay people in commune or community. The witness to Christ is borne alone on a hill-top or in the rush and scurry of the market-place. Both are really and truly Christian expressions. There is need, however, to approach the difference of life-styles soundly. Each will want to work according to its own pattern. Hence it is that many varied rules have been written, and especially many differing techniques of prayer are put forward as 'the way'.

INTRODUCTION

The value of the present book is just there. David Forrester simply, straightforwardly and with deep insights writes of the heart of the matter. He is concerned for the development of prayer and the life of union with Christ in the teeming world of every day. But there are two ways of approach. From the top it is possible to put principles and work down towards people: or we can start where people are and work from there, approaching the stage of principles by a more readily available route. The second incarnational method is used here.

Christ established incarnation as God's way of revealing himself finally. Can we do any better than follow his chosen way? He came to live among us. He was and is for everyone. Everyone is potentially available for the relationship with Jesus which leads to knowledge, love and service. This relationship is to grow and be developed in the only place where it naturally can develop ... where we are, here and now.

For the norm of today this means a situation of pressure from the world around. Particularly for the city-dweller there is an atmosphere of crowding, noise, tension. There is a draining concentration with a clamour of multiple distractions. All this disturbs our peace of mind and makes remote what is generally accepted as the atmosphere necessary for contemplation. Yet this is today's incarnational setting. This is real. It is here that the ordinary and average person is to meet God at that depth of intimacy in love which he uncovers for anyone who wants to fall and stay in love with him.

It is certainly true that there must be change in the world atmosphere, change in perspective and values. The mad scramble for material gain, cosiness in life, ever-increasing benefits and general permissiveness has to be tempered with understanding of true values and the quality of real love.

At the same time, it is not possible or good to await change, even if we are trying to bring it about. We must here and now live the values and the way because out of the tension and poverty of that very living will grow the spiritual power in you and me which will effect the eventual change. It is easy to dismiss this as pious talk. It is not just pious talk. Christ has given us the power through his Spirit. He has shown us the way. He witnessed to the possibility of being utterly godly in the place and at the time when he lived. The true peace and stillness of Christ were internal. He cut through noise, distractions and temptations to maintain an authority, calmness and vision which set his face for Jerusalem and all the suffering that meant. His example stands starkly but tranquilly as a model for us.

The important lessons from David Forrester's book are about our own nature and its reactions, about God's love especially for the poor, and about the possibility for each and every one of us to go forward in prayer and in love of God. Christ identified with the common man, and with those who were below the common man, the cripples, demented and wretched. If he was so concerned and so willing to love the outcast as well as his disciples, we have every hope if we want to make ourselves available for understanding with our hearts the measure of the Love who is Christ, Son of Man.

Michael Hollings

St Anselm's,
Southall, Middlesex
Feast of the Conversion of St Paul, 1978

Preface

Sooner or later these days, any priest working in a parish is approached by individuals or groups and asked to help them to pray. This short book is the product of trying over the years to meet this request.

In the past numerous works laid down what might loosely be termed the purpose and techniques of prayer. These were useful for those who led unhurried lives and had opportunities for leisure.

This book attempts to meet the needs, hopes and fears of people living often intensely occupied lives in the hustle and bustle of the twentieth century. It tries to present prayer as something challenging but within the grasp of us all, and as something closely linked with the kind of people we are and the life-style of most of us. It does not treat prayer as something esoteric or for specialists.

The book begins with a chapter on individual behaviour and moves to a Christian's place in society and the Church. It then attempts to guide the reader through consideration of various matters such as the value of silence, and how to cope with aging and loneliness, before reaching the main theme of listening with the heart; this is described in chapter seven. Chapter eight is an attempt to ground in Scripture all that has preceded it, and the final chapter shows how such prayer might be pursued in a group context.

No man is an island and clearly I have been influenced in writing this book by countless others. In particular I am deeply indebted to Michael Hollings. With much kicking and struggling on my part, it was he who many years ago first taught me the necessity of prayer. Later, his personal example had much to do with my offering myself for the priesthood. Today I am grateful for his continuing counsel and for writing the Introduction to this book.

To the girls of St Anne's Convent School, the parishioners of St Edmund's and the Sisters of Redcote Convent, all in Southampton, I owe much for their comments and criticisms.

Personal thanks are also due to Charles McCloskey for his encouragement and persistent badgering of me to put pen to paper.

I dedicate this book to my mother.

St Edward's, David Forrester
Chandler's Ford, Hampshire,

Feast of the Annunciation, 1978

I
Love and prayer

What is Christian love?
'To fall in love' is very simple. In theory it is possible to 'fall in love' with practically anything, but to love a person is not so easy. Indeed it may be very difficult.

The word 'love' is perhaps one of the most commonly used words in the English language. Don't we hear it everyday on pop records? Haven't we all at some time been called 'Love' by a bus conductress or a shop assistant? And when was the last time we said something like: 'Oh, I'd love a cup of tea' or 'I'd love to win the pools'? More importantly, can we remember the last time someone told us they loved us?

Clearly we use the word in many different ways. And yet unlike other things it never seems to bore us. Perhaps this is because the need and search for love is as much part of our nature as breathing, eating, drinking and sleeping. But just as we can breathe in bad air, eat poisoned food, drink sour milk or suffer from insomnia, isn't it equally possible for us to mistake some of our feelings for the genuine thing called love?

What do Christians mean by love? How should we in practice love our neighbour?

Obviously love shows itself in a variety of forms. That between a husband and wife is different from that between parents and children or brothers and sisters. Again it is not the same as love between friends. Nevertheless the genuine article has certain definite characteristics.

Normally when we think of people we know, we think of their appearance, character, habits or talents. Whenever we love someone, however, an inner or elusive quality in them becomes apparent to us. This is often puzzling or even amusing to others who do not see the hidden feature. How often we have heard the remark: 'I cannot for the life of me see what he sees in her!'

Moreover the discovery of this previously unknown side of another person is quite different from having sympathy, respect or even admiration for him or her. It might not in fact be much fun to love this person and perhaps even the contrary. If our feelings are not returned it can be painful. To become involved with another person can bring responsibilities and burdens. Even so, in loving another we overwhelmingly become more aware of a real and better self *within* ourselves (we speak of loving with all our heart). In other words, the act of loving brings out this other self. This is one of the signs that the love is genuine.

It is also quite apparent that real love is different from infatuation or 'calf love', and it is not simply physical desire — wanting to possess the other person.

Additionally, when a Christian says 'I love you' to someone, the 'you' must not be (if we are honest) a fantasy figure or a romantic idealization. Instead, it is this human being confronting us, compounded of good qualities and bad. To love someone means loving the whole person, but it does not imply giving uncritical approval to everything about the other. It is basically a will-to-do-good or as the Italians say: 'Ti voglio bene' — I want what is best for you.

From the stage of discovering that we love a person in this way and provided the feelings are mutual, we move imperceptibly to the stage of recognising not two persons — an 'I' and a 'You' — but an 'Us'. Sharing becomes second nature and the acquisition of each other's characteristics and habits is a common feature.

Nevertheless, there are always enemies of love to be kept at bay, such as possessiveness, jealousy, self-indulgence or taking the other for granted and seeking to dominate. Within a relationship of genuine love there should be mutual giving and receiving, communication, tolerance and constant purifying of one's motives. As St Paul told the Corinthians:

> Love is always patient and kind;
> it is never jealous;
> love is never boastful or conceited;
> it is never rude or selfish;
> it does not take offence, and is not resentful.
> Love takes no pleasure in other people's sins
> but delights in the truth;
> it is always ready to excuse, to trust, to hope,
> and to endure whatever comes. (1 Cor 13:4-7)

Love and friendship
Unlike love, friendship on the other hand is not instinctive, organic, biological or even strictly necessary. According to C.S. Lewis: 'It has least commerce with our nerves; there is nothing throaty about it; nothing that quickens the pulse or turns you red or pale.' What one notices most concerning people who are friends is that they are uninquisitive about each other, there is an equality between them, an openness in their relationship, and the question of duty does not enter their friendship.

Whereas lovers are often depicted as being absorbed in each other, friends share an interest in something other than themselves.

For the Christian, however, the test of whether his love is not counterfeit is the extent to which it incorporates these elements of friendship. If the Christian is loving authentically, then he will not spend his time gazing exclusively into his loved one's eyes. In other words, his human love should drive him on to the Eternal; to the God who first brought him and his loved one together in the first place. This is because the Christian is called upon to love both God and his neighbour.

In addition, at the Last Supper Jesus told his disciples: 'You are my friends if you do what I command you' (Jn 15:14). In other words, the Christian has the stupendous task and privilege of loving God and his neighbour and the opportunity of entering into friendship with Jesus.

But in practice how do we go about these things? In the first place, how we relate with our neighbour probably reveals how we approach God. At its best human love might be described as God's finger on man's shoulder. But how do we relate with others?

In regard to our family or friends, let alone our work associates or people in need, do we show our love by spending time with them, asking their advice, apologising when we are wrong, thanking them when they are kind, enjoying their company, and most of all listening to them? If we relate only badly in these ways with our neighbours, is it likely that our love for God is any different? Didn't St John say: 'Anyone who says, 'I love God' and hates his brother, is a liar, since a man who does not love the brother that he can see cannot love God whom he has never seen' (1 Jn 4:20)?

Love as service and sacrifice
If we have experienced what it means to will the good of another then this too might enable us to appreciate more fully why Christian love is often inseparable from service and sacrifice. We probably all know deep down that, whereas we can give without loving, it is not possible to love without giving. And haven't we all occasionally learnt the truth contained in the saying, 'I searched for my God and I could not find him. I looked for my soul and I could not find it. I searched for my brother and found all three'? Wasn't it from his own experience too that Albert Schweitzer was able to tell others: 'I don't know what your destiny will be, but one thing I know: the only ones among you who will be truly happy are those who will seek and find how to serve.'

This is poignantly illustrated in the story of the young man dying as told by Viktor Frankl in his book *Doctor and the Soul*. The young man had a tumour of the spine. At first glance he seemed just an ordinary person, but he knew he had not long to live. When he first entered hospital he quickly became the life and soul of his ward. He spent his days engaged in stimulating talk with the other patients — entertaining, encouraging and consoling them. He also especially enjoyed reading and listening to good music on the radio.

One day however the pain from his back hurt so much that it was too painful for him even to wear the head phones attached to the radio. His hands became so paralyzed that he could no longer hold books. The amazing thing was that even now the other patients continued coming to him for advice. Though he could not laugh or joke any more, he still listened to *their* problems and worries. He never once complained of his own pain and he became an example to all. Before he died the staff and the patients who had known this apparently ordinary young man had been taught what love is all about.

It is when one learns of people such as that young man that one can begin to understand what Gerald Vann meant when he wrote in *The Heart of Man*: 'Who is powerful, the man who can evict a thousand villagers from their homes or throw a million soldiers into the field and destroy a nation, or the man who can make a single human being give him his whole heart?'

Equally one can begin to grasp what St Teresa of Avila was getting at when she remarked of Christians who comprise the People of God, the Church: 'Christ has no body now on earth but your's; no hands but your's; your's are the eyes which see Christ's compassion for the world; your's are the feet through which he is to go about doing good; your's are the hands with which he is to bless men now'.

In the last analysis doesn't a Christian believe that 'a man can have no greater love than to lay down his life for his friends' (Jn 15:13)? And didn't Jesus also say, 'I give you a new commandment: love one another; just as I have loved you' (Jn 13:34)? Shouldn't giving therefore pervade every aspect of our lives? St Aelred of Rievaulx, who abandoned the court life of King David of Scotland to become a monk, surely appreciated this when he once prayed to God: 'What I feel, what I say, my leisure and my employment, what I do and what I think, my good fortune and my ill, my death and my life, my health and my sickness, whatever I am in any way, the fact that I live, feel, perceive, let it all be available *for them* and all be spent *for them* for whom you yourself did not disdain to be spent'.

Love and prayer
But what has loving to do with prayer? The answer is that before any of us can even aspire to reach the heights of love illustrated above, we need to understand the close connexion between love and prayer.

From where else other than from his loving and constant relation with his Father did Jesus derive his strength, sense of mission and inner peace? Why else should we read frequently in the Gospels that: 'Very early next morning he (Jesus) got up and went to a lonely spot and remained there in prayer' (Mk 1:35)? For what other reason than that the first and second commandments cannot be kept without recourse to prayer did St Paul so often instruct the early Christians to pray?

> 'Rejoice always, pray constantly, give thanks in all circumstances'. (1 Thess 5:16-18)
> 'Do not give up if trials come; and keep on praying'. (Rom 12:12)
> 'Pray all the time, asking for what you need praying in the Spirit on every possible occasion'. (Eph 6:18)

But how practicable is this for us living in the hectic twentieth century? When surrounded by crowds or caught up in traffic jams; at work on the factory floor or in the office poring over figures, hammering at typewriters and answering the telephone; coming home to houses with paper-thin walls and noisy neighbours; washing clothes, preparing meals, bathing the baby or seeing the children off to school; watching television or simply worrying about the mortgage and monthly bills, how can we pray as St Paul recommends?

The answer is that prayer for most of us is totally out of the question if it is viewed *solely* as an exercise requiring a great many words, instead of our being involved in a relationship of love with God. And therefore as in all matters of genuine love, won't there be ebbs and flows? This is surely part of the human condition? Since we are creatures with instincts and emotions as well as minds and wills, surely we should expect periods of dryness, monotony and fatigue as well as times of consolation, in our prayer lives as much as in our ordinary love lives?

Moreover, as St Thérèse of Lisieux once remarked: 'Souls vary as much as human faces'. In other words, no two people will ever pray in exactly the same way. But why should they? There is perhaps only one rule concerning prayer which applies to everyone and that is that we should pray as we are and where we are. This was a lesson learnt by the famous Jewish Rabbi, Zusyan. Zusyan sometimes wished he was someone other than himself. And then he always said to himself wisely: 'In the world to come they will not ask me, "Why were you not Moses?" They will ask: "Why were you not Zusyan?"'

In the presence of a loved one are we also never distracted, irritated, moody and talkative, as well as being able to enjoy periods of utter silence; a silence nevertheless which is not a vacuum but an occasion of intimate understanding too precious for words? Didn't Jesus himself say: 'In your prayers do not babble as the pagans do, for they think that by using many words they will make themselves heard' (Mt 6:7)? And if we are worn out, depressed, confused; if we are oppressed with worries and problems; doesn't God still love us and remain in our hearts?

Not long ago in a corridor of the underground of a foreign city a crowd was seen to gather round something on the ground. The people of this particular city are not renowned for their kindness or concern for others; beggars and crippled people are a familiar sight on most of the main streets and they are usually disregarded. The amazing thing then was that what had drawn the attention of the crowd were a young couple, sitting on the ground, clinging to each other.

Beside this obviously exhausted young man and woman was their story written in chalk. It said they were in their late twenties; they were husband and wife. The woman was three months pregnant and the man was a discharged convict, unable for the past year to obtain employment. They were literally on their last legs. They could no longer even beg in the ordinary way and simply sat there slumped and clinging to each other.

The crowd around them just stood there and looked in silence. But before most moved away, they left a token of money; something unusual in that city. How many of them realized that, amid our troubles or trials and the crises afflicting both the Church and the world today, God clings to each of us in the way that those two young people clung to each other? Wasn't that how Jesus described God the Father in the parable of the prodigal son?

> While he was still a long way off, his father saw him and was moved to pity. He ran to the boy, clasped him in his arms and kissed him tenderly (Lk 15:20).

Clearly then, Jesus is here showing us not only the nature and extent of God the Father's love for us but how often this relationship is expressed in ways other than words. The love between the father and the prodigal son was such that words were in a sense superfluous.

We have seen that in our relations with others, especially in the company of someone we love, we are often happiest being together in silence. And silence in these instances is the very opposite of emptiness.

In our prayer to God then should we not seek to arrive at a similar state? And at times when this is not practically possible, does this mean that God has ceased loving us? It might very well be the case that in fact we have been searching for God in the wrong places or, even more likely, failed to regard the circumstances of our times as especially suited to reaching God in prayer.

2
Trust in God alone

The challenge of the times
Paradoxically, the problems and pace of today's world which some Christians find upsetting and regard as obstacles in their prayer lives are precisely those which they should regard as both challenging and causes of celebration. If genuine prayer should not ever be divorced from our daily lives and our relations with others, perhaps it is time to see how even our worries can become a source of strength.

Isn't it possible that the trend of modern times for instance to undermine our ability to find security in worldly things, time-hallowed institutions or ourselves is actually an opportunity to throw ourselves totally on the mercy of God?

Isn't the present age with its daily record of violence, hunger and poverty, with its constant shadow of the possibility of a nuclear holocaust and with its failure to match its technological achievements with similar ones in the realm of human relationships, peace-keeping and justice, an excellent time for Christians to grasp the truth that, without reference to God, life on earth is meaningless?

Perhaps, indeed, never since the time when Christianity became the official religion of the Roman Empire in

312 AD, has the Church had such an opportunity to practise as well as preach the Gospel. Rarely before have *all* the people of God (as distinct from specific groups or individuals who from time to time suffered prejudice, persecution and martyrdom) had the chance to experience what it is to be counted among 'the poor of God'.

The poor of God
In the Old Testament the poor of God or the 'anawim' were those who, having been stripped of everything and sometimes sent into exile, came to place their hope and trust solely in God. They learnt the secret of power in weakness and glory through suffering (weakness in the sense of becoming pliant to God's ways, and suffering in the sense of dying to self). And they are depicted in the Psalms as beggars before God, the opposite of the proud and self-sufficient, to whom God is particularly close (Ps 21, 34 and 68).

It was of the 'anawim' that Jeremiah was speaking when he declared in whom God would put his law and write it upon their hearts; that Isaiah declared as the people to whom the Servant of the Lord, the Messiah, would come to preach the Good News; and that Ezekiel had in mind, albeit perhaps unconsciously, when he prophesied concerning those to whom God would give a new heart and a new spirit (Jer 31:33; Is 61:1; Ez 36:26). When we fret and become depressed about the state of the world, wouldn't it be useful then to see what we could learn by becoming 'the poor of God' ourselves?

One of the most typical of the poor of God in the New Testament was the Virgin Mary. Just as Hannah the mother of Samuel, another of the 'anawim' before her, Mary compressed her understanding of how 'God chooses the weak things of this world' (1 Cor 1:27) into her glorious Magnificat.

Nevertheless, we should never forget that though Mary did not hesitate to proclaim her faith that God was on the side of the humble and oppressed, this did not make her either proud or cringing. As Pope Paul has written in his moving document *To Honour Mary*: 'The modern woman will note with pleasant surprise that Mary of Nazareth while completely devoted to the will of God was far from being a timidly submissive woman or one whose piety was repellant to others ... The modern woman will recognise in Mary ... a woman of strength who experienced poverty, and suffering, flight and exile'.

We would perhaps appreciate this more if for a while we forgot the Mary we so often see depicted in pictures and statues. Instead it might be more helpful if we considered such facts as that she was probably a young girl of about fourteen when the Annunciation took place. It might assist us too to think of her as a typical young Jewess of her time, dark haired and of olive complexion, betrothed to Joseph a man much older than herself and a workman.

Have we any idea of the trauma it must have been for such a young woman to make the journey to Bethlehem in the middle of winter whilst she was pregnant and then to find there was nowhere to stay? And what must have been her thoughts as she fled into exile out of reach of the vengeful Herod? Even when Mary and Joseph were able to return home it was only to a small insignificant village, never once mentioned in the Old Testament. And as they lived there in obscurity, as the boy Jesus grew to manhood, may not Mary have been the victim of village gossip, a characteristic of small community life? If this is so, her trials would surely have increased when her son left home and began touring the countryside, preaching, teaching and performing miracles. Moreover, when her son was crucified as a common criminal where was she to be found but at the foot of the cross? Have we any conception of what she must have gone through?

Even so, it was her faith and trust in God that must have enabled her to keep going. And it was of such endurance and perseverance under strain that the 'anawim' were made. Small wonder that her cousin Elizabeth was able to greet her with the expression 'of all women you are the most blessed'. It was such people that Jesus also had in mind when he uttered the first of the Beatitudes: 'How happy are the poor in spirit; their's is the kingdom of heaven' (Mt 5:3).

Jesus as one of the poor of God

When thinking of Jesus as the Messiah who came to earth and fulfilled Isaiah's prophesy of a suffering servant, it is essential to see him as one of God's poor in the manner described above. Although he came as a king, it was not as the kind of king we usually imagine. When we consider monarchs we frequently think in terms of thrones, crowns, kingdoms, worldy authority and power. Jesus however was to shatter all these inadequate ideas as to what kingship meant.

His crown was made of thorns; his throne was a cross; his territory or kingdom was men's hearts and spirits; his power was that of being able to change men's hearts; his authority was that of reconciling mankind with his father. As St Paul was to write of Jesus: 'His state was divine, yet he did not cling to his equality with God but emptied himself to assume the condition of a slave, and became as men are; and being humbler yet, even to accepting death, death on a cross' (Phil 2:6-8).

Moreover it was with the insight of being a follower of such a Christ that St Paul could rejoice himself in his own suffering: ' "So I shall be very happy", Paul told the people of Corinth, "to make my weaknesses my special boast so that the power of Christ may stay over me, and that is why I am quite content with my weaknesses, and with insults, hardships, persecutions and with the agonies I go through for Christ's sake. For it is when I am weak that I am strong".'

When therefore we are concerned over such things as loss of status; when we place undue emphasis on man-made solutions to human problems and predicaments; and even when we cling blindly to past habits or practices in the Church (that is those originally only devised by past generations to suit their particular needs), then are we not letting slip the occasion to place all our trust in God alone?

Much of our trouble is that we are by nature comfort seeking creatures. By inclination we don't like facing problems or difficulties. We don't like dying to ourselves, being unselfish and emptied of self to give room for God. But if we loved someone sufficiently wouldn't we be prepared to do anything for them, so why not God? Perhaps as a people we wrap ourselves up in the flimsy garments of our own righteousness — and then too often complain of the cold! As the writer Carlo Falconi has observed: 'The reason why too many religious spirits wander endlessly along mistaken paths, victims of colossal and monstrous delusions, is that they choose to confuse ... *their* desires and aspirations with those of God. True religiousness ... consists essentially in putting oneself in the right place in relation to God, transforming one's own life into utterly *unselfish* service of Him'.

Suffering
The root of our unwillingness to die to self may be our fear of suffering. This is not to suggest that suffering is something to be sought or something noble in itself; when it comes in the shape of illness, injustice or poverty plain and simple then it needs to be combatted. But when it is inescapable and might be termed one of the inexorable 'givens' of life, then have we any right to shrink from it when Christ has known what it is before us and he has promised us the Holy Spirit to comfort us in our hour of trial? Isn't it possible too as we are often reminded: 'The human heart has places that do not exist and into them enters suffering that they may exist'?

So how should the Christian behave in the face of suffering and hardship, even as is most likely it comes only in the shape of unkindness at the hands of others, gossip, envy, disregard of our feelings or views, disputes at work, differences with colleagues and so on? Shouldn't we remember the words of Jesus: 'Come to me all you who labour and are overburdened, and I will give you rest'? And couldn't we find solace in the psalmist's song:

> Rest in God alone, my soul!
> > He is the source of my hope;
> with him alone for my rock, my safety,
> > my fortress, I can never fall;
> rest in God, my safety, my glory,
> > the rock of my strength? (Ps 62)

Just as earlier we remarked that how we love might show us how we pray, so might how we regard the world. If we are not loving others as we should, our relation with God in prayer will be inadequate, no matter how much we may think otherwise. If too we are pessimistic about the state of the world and vainly imagine that all its problems would be resolved if man would only work at them himself, so we are far from being 'the poor of God'. And it is the people who put their whole trust in God alone who, according to Jesus, are members of his kingdom.

This being the case, it is equally important that the Church, the people of God, should discover its true rôle in modern society and especially by reading the signs of the times.

3
Christians as seed in the earth

The role of the Church
In a world beset by enormous problems, characterized by constant change and subject to pressure from political power blocs and bureaucracies, the individual often feels helpless. Pained by reading of human affliction or watching on television the sufferings of his fellow creatures at home and overseas whenever a civil war occurs, a high-jacking takes place, unemployment mounts or an earthquake, famine, disease or monsoon strikes, he considers there is little he can personally do about this state of affairs. More often than not, believing himself to be impotent, he either becomes indifferent or retreats into nostalgia about the past.

How frequently do we not hear that western society is breaking down? Is it not constantly suggested that not only do young people no longer respect their elders, but that family life, morals and standards are fast disappearing?

Whilst not denying that there is ample evidence to support such arguments, it is equally possible to produce evidence to the contrary. In fields such as care for the aged, penal reform, child care, medicine and educational opportunities — to name just a few — the changes for the good in the period since the end of World War II have to be balanced against the evils of the present permissive and post-Christian society.

When it comes to considering the Church, equally it is necessary to take a balanced view before assessing what has happened in recent times. Whether a Christian is by temperament and attitude inclined to rejoice over or regret the apparent loss of prestige of the Church in modern times, at least he cannot fool himself that this fact alone does not compel the Church to play a different rôle in society from former times.

In place of outward triumphalism the Church has now to concentrate on revealing its inner nature as 'a kind of sacrament or sign of intimate union with God, and of the unity of mankind'. 'It is not set up to seek earthly glory, but to proclaim humility and self-sacrifice, even by its own example.'

Called to live in the world but not to be of it, individual Christians too have the vital task of not witnessing to their numerical strength and world influence but to the eternal value and relevance of the Good News. Scattered in the world they are called upon even more today to be what Bishop John Taylor of Winchester in his book *The Go-Between God* describes as 'like seed in the earth, salt in the stew, yeast in the dough'.

Even with this vocation of sacrifice to which the Church and the people who comprise it are called, it is however still too easy to settle for half measures. It may be the case indeed that we are often too frightened to face up to what God is actually asking of us at this particular point in time. The habit of centuries of power and influence is hard to throw off, and in any case 'it is a dreadful thing to fall into the hands of the living God' (Heb 10:31). Have we the courage to be as the 'anawin'?

Obviously the Christian in the world is called upon at

all times to defend as strongly as he can values which are fundamental such as the right to live and the equality of all men before God regardless of colour, race or creed. Equally he is bound to support ceaselessly causes which either alleviate human suffering or which seek to promote justice. The commandment to love our neighbour is unending.

Nevertheless, activity of itself is not enough. Even Jesus used every act of healing and miracle not merely to bring relief, but to teach the truths of the kingdom of God.

The place of the cross
In seeking to promote love and brotherhood, however, it is still possible for us to hide from the cross in Christian living. How many of us flee from the call to take up our own cross by filling our days with good works? Do we ignore Christ's words that 'unless a wheat grain falls on the ground and dies, it remains only a single grain'?

It is a standing temptation for the unhappy priest or the frustrated lay person to plunge into intense activity. We each have a wardrobe of disguises to conceal our real selves in other spheres. How often does not a forthright manner cloak an inner hesitancy; an impatience with demonstrations of affection mask a desire for love; and a pretended indifference hide a painful sensitivity? Just as much then we may flee from problems into action. But just as it is necessary for us to understand more fully as Christians our calling to be the poor of God and to be stripped of the vestiges of triumphalism, so we have to accept like St Paul that God's ways are not necessarily man's ways:

> 'The language of the cross', St Paul told the people of Corinth, 'may be illogical to those who are not on the

way to salvation, but those of us who are on the way see it as God's power to save. As scripture says: I shall destroy the wisdom of the wise and bring to nothing all the learning of the learned ... And so, while the Jews demand miracles and the Greeks look for wisdom, here are we preaching a crucified Christ; to the Jews an obstacle that they cannot get over, to the pagans madness, but to those who have been called, whether they are Jews or Greeks, a Christ who is the power and the wisdom of God. For God's foolishness is wiser than human wisdom, and God's weakness is stronger than human strength' (1 Cor 1: 18-25).

Equally, we have to accept that God invariably uses human reverses and failure as the means to show us that only through him shall man be made whole.

A Christian should not seek success for its own sake, if only because his view point should extend further. If success comes his way then he has the added task of not crediting it to himself.

For a Christian, whatever good occurs in this life is essentially a gift from God, a preparation for and foretaste of what is to come and what we now see only darkly. 'We are only the earthenware jars', says St Paul, 'that holds this treasure, to make it clear that such an overwhelming power comes from God and not from us' (2 Cor 4:7). We are after all a people in pilgrimage, following a leader who suffered and died the death of a common criminal.

How then can the Church ensure that it continually remembers its proper role? And just as much, how can we who make up the Church not fall into the trap of seeking solace in transitory things? Most important of all, how can we expel doubt and fear in ourselves and at the same time be a source of encouragement and inspiration to those around us? Yet again it is incumbent on the people of God to follow the example of St Paul:

> We are in difficulties on all sides, but never cornered; we see no answer to our problems, but never despair; we have been persecuted, but never deserted; knocked down, but never killed; always, wherever we may be, we carry with us in our body the death of Jesus, so that the life of Jesus, too, may always be seen in our body. Indeed, while we are still alive, we are consigned to our death every day, for the sake of Jesus, so that in our mortal flesh the life of Jesus, too, may be openly shown (2 Cor 4:8-12).

If however we are to pursue the way of the cross effectively, it is time we considered the value of silence and simplicity in prayer which are both essential to 'listening with the heart'.

4
The value of silence and simplicity in prayer

The need for silence
In a society full of noise, bustle, speed and crises there is always the danger of losing or even of ignoring our bearings. What we desperately need today, especially if we are active in the world, is to heed the words of such people as the Syrian monk, Isaac of Nineveh:

> Many are avidly seeking but they alone find who remain in continual silence ... Every man who delights in a multitude of words, even though he says admirable things, is empty within. If you love truth, be a lover of silence. Silence like the sunlight will illuminate you in God and will deliver you from the phantoms of ignorance. Silence will unite you to God himself ...
> More than all things love silence: it brings you a fruit that tongue cannot describe. In the beginning we have to force ourselves to be silent. But then there is born something that draws us to silence. May God give you an experience of this 'something' that is born of silence. If you only practise this, untold light will dawn on you in consequence ... After a while a certain sweetness is born in the heart of this exercise

and the body is drawn almost by force to remain in silence.

Moreover this silence is available to all men and women. It is dependent neither on intelligence nor on having a strong intellect. Archbishop Anthony Bloom makes this clear in a story he tells in his book *School for Prayer* of an old lady who came to him for advice. Although she had been praying continuously for fourteen years, she had never sensed the presence of God. The Archbishop gave her counsel and subsequently she told him what happened as a result.

On arriving home she had gone to her room, made herself comfortable and had begun to knit. She felt relaxed and observed with content what a nice shaped room she had, with its view of the garden and the sound of her needles hitting the arm of her chair. And then gradually she became aware that the silence was not simply the absence of sound, but was filled with its own density. 'And', she said, 'it began to pervade me. The silence around began to come and meet the silence in me ... All of a sudden I perceived that the silence was a presence. At the heart of the silence there was Him'.

When thinking on this story it is important to note that the old lady had been praying continuously for fourteen years before she experienced what can occur in the depths of silence. In order to open one's self up to this, to finding in silence not a mere absence of noise but the presence of God, it is usually the case that much preparation is called for.

How to achieve inner silence
In the first place we have to be prepared to lay aside a certain amount of time each day for prayer — and persevere no matter how difficult this may prove to be.

The discovery of God's presence in silence also presupposes that we do not ever neglect the usual, every day and normal opportunities of communicating with him.

In other words, what might be termed formal and communal prayer is maintained to the point of becoming the bedrock of personal prayer. Whether such prayer consists of praise and thanksgiving, petition or sorrow, whether it be said spontaneously or in words familiar to all such as the Our Father, and whether it be said or sung as may be the Psalms, it should have become second nature to us. Just as we would only foolishly neglect to go for long without food, sleep or sufficient oxygen, so formal prayer and frequenting the sacraments should become a staple ingredient of a regular diet.

Similarly an encounter with God in silence is rarely attained unless we have also deliberately sought him at all times elsewhere. In our dealings with others, in the routine of our daily life, in the monotony and possible fatigue of our work, and in such apparently mundane things as listening to the radio, watching television or reading newspapers, do we inwardly reflect on what God is making of it all? Whenever as Christians we turn to the Bible, do we approach it on the level of personal involvement, laying ourselves open to being provoked, possibly judged and criticised by what lies before us? Or do we read it as a duty and as something slightly removed from our twentieth century mentality, forgetting that the Word of God is for all men, at all times and everywhere?

Undeniably it is extremely difficult to achieve silence even in the heart of the country and away from the constant cacophony of noise inseparable from modern urban life. Even when we are far removed from other people, thoughts move restlessly through our heads like the buzzing of flies (Bishop Theopan) or the inexplicable leaping of monkeys from branch to branch (Ramakrishna) for, as St Mark the monk once observed: 'The rational mind cannot rest idle'. And even if it were possible for rational thinking to be silenced, we would then have our imaginations to contend with. So what is the solution?

How to simplify our prayer
One of the things which we can do is to simplify our personal prayer by continually uttering a short formula of prayer, or even one word redolent in Christian overtones and tradition. Our minds will rarely in the beginning cease being plagued by other concerns, but they will gradually become subdued.

The 'laying aside' of thought by the continuous utterance of such formulae as 'Lord Jesus, Son of God, have mercy on me a sinner', or of such words as 'Love', 'Peace' or 'Holy', is not an exercise in repression or furious conflict, but a quiet and gentle process, albeit requiring absolute perseverance. It is akin to sweeping a room clean, regularly and rhythmically; clean of furniture, pictures and clutter. On the other hand it is decidedly not quietist which implies passivity, but a process requiring constant vigilance, attentiveness and above all the quality of 'listening'. Moreover it can be pursued wherever a Christian may be. Whether he be travelling on a bus or train, waiting for either, walking down a high street, or cooking a meal at home, the aim is to increase an awareness of God's presence. In time it may also coincide with the rhythm of one's breathing and be as natural.

Paradoxically, this 'laying aside' of thought and images ultimately increases one's awareness of the value of all things and persons in God. Not merely do we come to see ourselves in relation to God but everyone and thing besides. As the anonymous Russian peasant and author of *The Way of the Pilgrim* states:

> When ... I prayed with all my heart, everything around me seemed delightful and marvellous. The trees, the grass, the birds, the earth, the air and the light seemed to be telling me that they existed for man's sake, that they witnessed to the love of God for man, that all things prayed to God and sang his praise ... Again I started off on my wanderings. But now I did not walk along as before, filled with care. The invocation of the Name of Jesus gladdened my way. Every body was kind to me, it was as though everyone loved me ... If anyone harms me I have only to think, 'How sweet is the Prayer of Jesus!' and the injury and anger pass away and I forget it all.

The prayer then that issues from the interior silence described above is something which flows naturally and simply. Its source is that personal region beyond the areas open to analysis, where God is 'more intimate to us than we are to ourselves' (Augustine). It is here too that a Christian faces up to his own unworthiness and utter dependence on God; realities which rule out any chance of indulging in self-glorification. It is here that he will discover – in an unending pilgrimage of discovery – the God who gives meaning and purpose to life, including that of the feverish present.

The need for interior peace
Not long ago three members of a family went to visit a relative who was a resident in an institution for the mentally handicapped. When they first arrived they

were rather frightened to find themselves sitting in a lounge with about thirty other people, all of whom were either blind, unable to stand or walk properly, unable to eat or go to the lavatory without assistance or who spoke in the language of children even though many of them were quite old. What made the visitors' experience more frightening was that during the two hours they were there no other visitors came to the home.

It was during the passage of those two hours however that something remarkable happened. The visitors only realised it once they had driven away. In place of their initial fear of the unknown and unexpected, the distressing and the sad, each of them experienced a profound sense of peace. So strong was this feeling that as they journeyed home they asked each other what they had felt about the visit.

The first said that he had been made to feel acutely aware of his own blessings (and this was said by a man who has only one leg and one lung). The second visitor remarked that she had felt a tremendous compassion come over her; she had wanted to share in the companionship of the handicapped people she had encountered. But the third member of the family said that he had felt himself in the presence of something special.

It was this last remark which struck them all and enabled them to understand why they had each been impressed without being able adequately to put it into words. None of the people they had seen and whom any of us normally would have considered 'handicapped' had any thought except to be themselves. The things which we and the visitors to the institution usually bother about so much — money, status, pleasure or even concern for our rights — meant nothing to the people living in that home. This proved to be the source of their peace and what had communicated itself to the visitors. It made the latter wonder who in fact were really handicapped — the inmates of the home or themselves?

Such a sense of peace at the centre of a meeting is not therefore unknown to us. Haven't we often heard the legend of the meeting between St Francis of Assisi and St Dominic? Apparently they met, they embraced, said nothing and went their separate ways but even so they understood each other perfectly. This kind of silence which is accompanied by interior peace is indeed at the heart of some of our deepest encounters; words prove either out of place or inadequate, something totally unnecessary. On occasion it may even be a source of wonder to others as well as oneself: 'And Pilate again asked Jesus, "Have you no answer to make?" "See how many charges they bring against you." But Jesus made no further answer, so that Pilate wondered' (Mk 15).

In the face of accusations, insinuations, calumnies or down right lies, often our only course is to remain silent. But in the meeting between Jesus and Pilate was it only Jesus' silence that made Pilate wonder. Wasn't he also perhaps being taught that the sort of silence which emanates from deep interior peace may often be the answer demanded by truth?

Speech does not in fact always bear witness; it is a fallacy to believe that 'getting it off one's chest' is always right. Genuine silence may also proclaim that truth is not in the last analysis an idea or a proposition but a reality greater than any argument or matter of speech. And it is especially genuine when it is the product of simple prayer and when it coincides with interior peace.

5
Human growth and prayer

Unity in man's make-up
The cultivation of silence, simple prayer and inner peace, although taking place within the interior of a Christian, is never at odds with his external activity, his every day life or duties. Much of our confusion, frustration, and even loss of direction stems from the distinction we falsely make and imagine exists in our make-up between the 'spiritual' and the 'secular'. In fact the two should be incapable of separation in the sense that the former should constantly be informing, moulding and shaping the latter. What takes place as a result of our cultivation of silence and continuous dialogue with God in our depths should bear fruit in our daily routine, in the work in which we are involved, in the quality of our family life and in the fostering of friendships.

Happily we are gradually returning to the Hebrew understanding of the fundamental unity in man's make-up; the knowledge that in man his mind, body and spirit consist of a whole and that to neglect one aspect of his person will have adverse effects in others. This is especially so for each of us on the path to maturity.

Maturity is clearly dependent in the initial stages on such factors as heredity, but don't Christians also hold that God knew them even before they were formed in the womb? Isn't it somewhat myopic too if we ignore his influence as we develop towards adulthood?

From birth to adulthood
Broadly speaking, it is clear that in our progress from birth to maturity we all as individuals pass through different stages of growth. Our very early childhood, when we were immersed in our immediate environment, was essentially restricted to bodily needs and communication; the need to touch, obtain food, warmth and protection were our prime concerns. We were totally unable to separate our existence from that of things and other people; our mother's presence (or absence) was of crucial importance.

In the third or fourth month after our birth our own persons became the centre of our conscious lives; the beginnings of separation set in and we were inclined to desire other things and people for what they were able to give us. Even in childhood, as opposed to babyhood, this process may have persisted (it would have been unnatural had it not) and we may have been inclined to be self-regarding, narcissistic, possibly precocious or given to tantrums.

Even without taking into account our physical environment, the social conditions in which we lived, the elementary and primary education we may have received, it is obvious that the attitudes of our parents towards us at this stage was crucial. Could they be depended upon to give us security and trust? Did they accept us completely? Were they to be relied upon to be predictable in their attitudes towards us? And if they were not, who can claim to have developed during these years totally unscathed?

But if we were incorporated by baptism into Christ's

body, the Church, and had been given the gift of the indwelling of the Holy Spirit in our infancy, wouldn't this have given us the opportunity of growing more effectively?

> People even brought little children to Jesus, for him to touch them; but when the disciples saw this they turned them away. But Jesus called the children to him and said, 'Let the little children come to me and do not stop them; for it is to such as these that the kingdom of God belongs. I tell you solemnly, anyone who does not welcome the kingdom of God like a little child will never enter it' (Lk 18: 15-17).

Is there any one of us who can accurately estimate the effect and value of bringing a child to Jesus for him to 'touch' him?

Nevertheless, whatever the nature of our most early experiences, we still all had the well known features if not trauma of adolescence to negotiate before we could hope to be considered mature human beings. It was then that each of us underwent fundamental physical, emotional and sexual growth. Was such growth however matched in our understanding and love of God?

This was the period when we possibly strove to achieve our own identity or learnt for the first time what it meant to be alone. We began to recognise the distinctive features of our own personalities. We perhaps also first appreciated or were bewildered by the fact that the different aspects in our nature (mental, physical and spiritual) were not merely related but were in some indefinable sense incapable of separation.

When our bodies were tired we learnt that we could not think clearly. On the occasions when we were emotionally upset our bodies were affected, if not made to feel sick. How often was it that our sexual urges failed to convey love? We discovered indeed that in a very real sense there is a unity in man, but often its parts were at war with each other. Didn't the meaning of St Paul's words come home to us for perhaps the first of many subsequent times?

> The fact is, I know of nothing good living in me, that is, in my unspiritual self, for though the will to do what is good is in me, the performance is not, with the result that instead of doing the good things I want to do, I carry out the sinful things I do not want. When I act against my will, then, it is not my true self doing it, but sin which lives in me.
>
> In fact this seems to be the rule, that every single time I want to do good it is something evil that comes to hand. In my inmost self I dearly love God's Law, but I can see that my body follows a different law that battles against the law which my reason dictates (Rom 7:18-23).

In sometimes failing therefore to listen to our true and inmost selves, what happened to our relationship with Christ at this stage of our growth? Did we find the guidance to restore the sense of friendship and love we had with him from baptism, or did misfortunes, betrayals and fear of commitment elsewhere cause us to let it wither? Did we seek reconciliation and strength in Holy Communion or did we drift away from the sacraments?

Our mentors may have informed us that maturity consists in such things as being able to be absorbed in a subject to the exclusion of ourselves; to be able to defend ourselves in conflict and to laugh at ourselves; to see ourselves objectively when need be; and to be able to commit ourselves to an ideal or to another person for life. But how many of us achieved this — if at all — unaided and without regression? Did we recognise the truth of the Vatican II statement that 'Whoever follows after Christ, the perfect man, becomes himself more a man'?

Perhaps it would have been more obvious if the Church could more clearly be seen to be ministering to our growth as persons and if grace were to be viewed as God's presence in our hearts. It would then be even more the rôle of the Church, in assisting the growth of Christians to maturity, to encourage in us the sense of 'openness' — to God at our centre, to others, and to fundamental aspects of life such as recognising our utter dependence on God, our need for love and the positive value of following in the steps of Jesus. We should also endeavour to make our own the prayer of St Paul for the people of Ephesus: 'Out of his infinite glory, may God give you the power through his spirit for your hidden self to grow strong, so that Christ may live in your hearts through faith . . .'

Nevertheless, and if only falteringly we attain to adulthood with the assistance of the Holy Spirit, it then becomes necessary to face without fear the stages of middle and old age and the problems they bring with them.

Crises in later life
Growing old is not something we like to think about. If we are already middle aged or approaching retirement it may be a subject we even dread. Who is unafraid of the possibility of becoming frail, sick, dependent on others, experiencing the loss of friends and former colleagues through death and of ending our own days either in a home or as the responsibility of others?

> She gets up at 5 a.m., not because she has a lot to do but because she has nothing to do. She can't sleep longer because she had nothing to do yesterday either. By 9.30 p.m. she is so weary of television or silence that she goes to bed, her eyes tired, her arthritic joints paining, and her system unready for sleep.

This description of an old woman by the author Dolores Curran probably fits that of countless old folk in our society today, not to mention the 22,000 mentally confused old people who are moved from their homes to hospitals each year. But the problem of aging is not something which comes upon us suddenly. Most of us recognise its approach at about the age of forty and during the subsequent period known as middle age.

For those with resources of intellect and personality, the time when they are between forty and sixty may be regarded as years of challenge. For the majority however it is a stage when anxiety and fears for the future begin to set in.

In the case of men there may be problems associated with progress in their careers and the dispersal of children from the home. For women during middle age the menopause puts an end to their reproductive life and they are thereby given physical proof of their growing old. And if we consider solely the medical and psychological data associated with our later life, it is small wonder that it is a subject we fear.

What men like to know that in their late fifties they will be able to do hard physical work at only about sixty percent of the rate possible ten years previously? Is the fact that coronary troubles are a common feature for men between forty and fifty something pleasant for them to think about? Would either sex welcome the knowledge that between fifty and sixty there is an increased incidence of alcoholism, depressive illness and stress disorders? Who enjoys learning that hearing and sight deteriorate as age advances? And who is not aware, albeit secretly, that retirement at sixty-five and with it the opportunity no longer of earning money brings its own particular fears? No one likes the labels frequently attached to old age, such as the elderly being less available and more diminished, depleted, withdrawn, constricted and even withered. So what should be the Christian approach to increasing old age? Much, if not all, may well depend on how truly we coped with earlier crises in our lives, realised our potential when moving towards adulthood and, above all, related to God in prayer. This is clear in the examples of two eighty-year old women, one formerly a celebrated local councillor in a large city and the other a nun who had held the highest positions of authority in her religious order.

Finding God
In the case of the councillor, during her active public life which lasted sixty years she had been held in high regard not only because of her position, but because of the number who had relied upon her services. When age took its toll and she was forced through ill health to retire, she found it difficult to adjust to her new rôle. Instead of being depended upon she became dependent on others; instead of leading an active life she became increasingly immobile through arthritis and slight heart failure; instead of resting secure in her position she found that others soon either forgot her or had little time for her. Ultimately isolated, she spent her final days bitterly recalling her past efforts on behalf of others; unable to come to terms with her changed

circumstances, she behaved as a recluse wrapt up in herself.

The elderly nun on the other hand, when forced to retire, eagerly grasped her remaining years as an opportunity to deepen her relationship with God in prayer. Instead of resting on her laurels, she made God and prayer her full time occupation until her death. This not only gave her a sense of purpose and belonging, but lent inspiration to those around her. Her final years were not therefore years of disengagement but of integration into the life of the community around her, even though she was experiencing bodily deterioration and was physically dependent on others. And the source of her ability to adjust and fulfil a meaningful rôle to the end of her life was her relationship with God, often pursued in silence but imbued with interior peace and expressed in love and concern for others.

Whereas the former councillor died lonely and unmourned, the elderly nun never knew loneliness, though she had often quoted John Milton's words for the benefit of others to the effect that loneliness was 'the first thing which God's eye named not good'.

6
Prayer as a solution to loneliness

Causes of loneliness
It is commonplace today to hear much about how the three processes of industrialization, urbanization and secularization have contributed to making loneliness an escalating problem of our times. In particular our attention is often drawn to the fact that most people nowadays no longer live and work in the same area. We rarely walk (even around our neighbourhood) but drive and thereby inhibit commerce with our neighbours. The nuclear family, because it lacks extensions close at hand in the shape of other relatives, frequently intensifies tensions and loneliness in the home.

Monotony and routine on factory floors also get blamed for the incidence of loneliness. Reference is sometimes made too to the fact that the jargon and language of technology restrict the communication of any job satisfaction we might be experiencing, so our families and friends sometimes feel 'left out' of a large part of our lives.

Critics of high-rise flats and 'concrete jungles', advocates of good neighbourhood schemes or commune living, pundits of the decline of institutional religion naturally all produce their reasons for loneliness. And amid all the often laudable uproar of the sociologists, part familiar and part sentimental, it seems almost a shame to ask whether we are perhaps missing the point?

Is loneliness truly an escalating problem of our times? Isn't it an experience known to every period of history and culture and the only difference is that today we are more aware of it? For the discovery of its manifold causes and its alleviation, shouldn't we do more than simply, albeit enjoyably, let off an immense volume of steam? Shouldn't we first examine ourselves? Might not this enable us also to reach to the heart of our being where God exists? Yet again however this would require that we cultivate the 'openness' spoken of earlier.

Flights from loneliness
Unfortunately, many of us are afraid to be 'open' and consequently suffer the loneliness so much debated. In many cases though this is not immediately apparent to others or admitted to ourselves, so skilful are our flights from reality or our adoption of poses. How many of us are discerning enough about ourselves or our friends to recognise the true use of leisure for example from escapism?

How many people do we know who hide from loneliness in over-eating, over-drinking or over-sleeping? How often do we avoid a problem by indulging in the feverish activity mentioned earlier and refusing to sit still? Haven't we all at some stage given way to day-dreams, even though they may not have reached the proportions of Walter Mitty's? Our disguises in the face of others may be even more ingeniously contrived.

Since the time of Pelagius, the British monk of the early fifth century, who taught that man took the initial and fundamental step towards salvation by his own efforts without the aid of God, it may have been an especially English failing to pretend that as individuals we are utterly self-sufficient. We have often been inculcated with the belief that we should take pride in standing on our own feet. In reality and beneath (to others) our perhaps daunting external behaviour, we may be highly sensitive and easily hurt.

How often does an aggressive manner conceal a deeper shyness and hesitant nature? Doesn't the dislike of the mention of death conceal a wish not even to think about it? Are not the 'lady-killers' in our midst in fact incapable of forming stable relationships and therefore 'lost' in their emotional immaturity?

What of those who, in moments of crisis or panic, assert supposed rights irrelevant to the matter in hand? What are the root causes of frequent name dropping if not basic insecurity?

Clearly too one does not have to live alone in order to suffer loneliness. It is not a simple problem confined to the elderly retired in our cathedral cities or south-coast resorts. And the non-communication which sometimes exists within families is not always a question of the generation gap.

Haven't we all encountered husbands who 'flee' from their wives into hobbies or who plead pressures of work to avoid coming home on time, and wives who 'busy' themselves with the children or domestic pursuits in order to escape from the loneliness of their marriage? What about the couples who concentrate so much on their children that, when the offspring are older and preparing to leave home, the parents are worried about what will keep them together?

Such flights and poses may indeed be necessary safety-valves in a given situation, but nevertheless they are the antithesis of openness and are therefore impediments to any growth in our relationship with God and others. Just as the child needs affection from its parents, so adults need acceptance by their peers. In extreme cases loneliness gives way to isolation and, as Erich Fromm the eminent psychologist has warned: 'To feel completely isolated leads to mental disintegration just as physical starvation leads to death'. The monk Hubert Van Zeller summed up the state of loneliness when he wrote:

> To be cut off from other human beings
>   and their love,
> to be cut off from all sense of God
>   and of his love,
> to be cut off from what one believes
>   to be one's real self
> and to be lodged in the body of a ghost
>   who has lost the power to love:
> this is loneliness.

How to overcome loneliness
What practical steps, then, can we take to achieve a greater degree of openness and exorcise loneliness from our individual lives? What is required to lead us to our true selves whom only God knows and understands completely, but who is ever ready to assist us if we would only listen with our hearts?

The first requirement would seem to be that we should take stock of our own flights and poses and accept them for what they are — escapes from reality. Unless in a sense we peel away the masks and subterfuges (often of our own devising) which surround what St Paul describes as our true and inmost selves, how else can we hope to know who we really are? Equally important, until we are able to approach the ultimate region in ourselves which is beyond the reach of ordinary analysis, how can we tell that we are actually meeting God and listening to him there with our heart? It is only when we choose to live with our more superficial selves after all that we experience loneliness.

What we therefore need is the much misunderstood and underestimated virtue known as humility. This actually means genuine self-knowledge, the acceptance of our good and bad points, the recognition of our true abilities and limitations, and the refusal to reach for things beyond our grasp. Above all we have to cease thinking in terms of our own self-sufficiency.

Dag Hammarskjöld was of the opinion that the Christian should pray that any loneliness he may be feeling might be a spur into finding something to live for and something great enough to die for. This will not be discovered however until a Christian has begun listening with the heart in silence where the author of all meaning is to be found in each one of us.

7
Listening with the heart in prayer

What is listening with the heart?
For a Christian in modern society what does it mean to cultivate listening with the heart? Basically it involves emulating St Catherine of Siena who, after three years of prayer in the solitude of her room at home, was commanded by Christ to engage in a life of action and apostolic works but to maintain her close relationship with him by carrying her monastic cell around *within* her. Reluctant at first to abandon her hermit-like life where she had learnt so remarkably how to listen to the promptings of God with her heart, Catherine soon discovered that action and continuous awareness of God's presence within her were not in fact incompatible.

This immediately suggests that listening with the heart is not the same thing as being introspective. Essentially it is not constant preoccupation with one's own thoughts, concerns and desires, but the arrival at a state of being at the deepest level of self, beyond such matters. It is the point attained after one has been stripped clean of one's outer shells which we often confuse with the real self. No longer bothered about oneself or with projecting this supposed picture of oneself to the rest of the world, one's main concern is simply to do the will of God discovered at one's centre in silence.

Moreover this is not to be confused with an exploration of one's unconscious. It is much more akin to the experience described by St Augustine in his Confessions, when he tells how 'the mysterious eye of his soul gazed on the light that never changes; above the eye of the soul, and above intelligence'.

In other words, it means finding ourselves with and in Christ; experiencing rather than debating the Christian realities of our existence and encountering God at the core of our being. At the same time, listening with the heart is not a matter of acquiring a technique (useful though such things may be by way of preparation) so much as a movement of the will in the direction of surrender, coupled with a deep conviction of the efficacy of faith. 'I tell you most solemnly, anything you ask for from the Father he will grant in my name' (Jn 16:23).

Tests of authenticity
But how accurately can we assess whether or not we have reached our inmost true selves and actually are listening with the heart?

One sure sign is that we are at peace with God. This is not the same thing as saying we are necessarily and outwardly at peace with ourselves! The nature of the peace experienced when one has taken to heart the words 'be still and know that I am God' has been described in down to earth language by Abbot John Chapman in his *Spiritual Letters:*

> It is not a peace which is *felt* (emotionally, sensibly), but supersensible. If you try to translate it into language, you may find yourself saying something

like this: — 'What *does* it all matter? What does it matter whether I enjoy Mass, or feel distracted or annoyed? What do my feelings matter? I came here for God, not for myself. What do *I* matter? Only God matters. The whole world doesn't matter. Glory to God, that is the whole of everything.'

And you look down at your soul, with a sort of amused pity, as a little wriggling worm, that won't keep still.

The importance of attaining such interior peace is forcibly illustrated in connexion with the Sabbath. Among the Jews at the time of Christ and still today the Sabbath might be described as the most outstanding phenomenon of their religion. For the Jews the Sabbath was and is regarded as *the* sign between them and God (Ex 31:17). Its traditional name is 'Yom Menuhah' which means day of rest. (It is akin to the 'still waters' mentioned in Psalm 23.) And this expression 'Yom Menuhah' is not intended to imply something purely passive, a stoppage of labour or the taking of a break. It is considered a symbolic freeing of the person from the chains of time which are experienced wherever there is change. The Sabbath in other words expresses the idea of complete harmony between man and nature, and man and man. This is very different from simple relaxation and taking things easy. If change can symbolically be eradicated by a person ceasing from work or doing anything which disturbs the notion of timelessness, then it is held that the Sabbath is paradise in miniature. Hence we have the notion expressed in Jewish folklore that if every Jew in the world were to keep the Sabbath as he is supposed to, then the Messiah would come.

When we read of the conflict — often bitter — between

Jesus and the pharisees on this question of the Sabbath, we are often unaware of the implications behind it. We fail to understand why the pharisees were so intransigent if not pedantic on the matter of breaking the Sabbath.

What they too in their turn failed to understand was that though Jesus fully approved of the idea behind the institution of the Sabbath, he elevated it and interiorized it. When he declared that 'The Son of Man is master even of the Sabbath', Jesus was not only making a proclamation about himself but he was trying to indicate that a real Sabbath is something best cultivated within us. It is an interior peace and harmony that he was attempting to inculcate in his listeners.

When he appeared to his disciples after the Resurrection he again was to emphasize the value of such peace by repeating the greeting 'Peace be with you' three times. Moreover he breathed on them. Such was the peace that enabled his disciples to be seen as different from other kinds of people, for in breathing on them Jesus bestowed the gift of the Holy Spirit. Whenever we experience this same kind of interior peace, we can be sure that we are listening with the heart.

Later on in the same letter of Abbot Chapman quoted earlier we find reference to the second sign of whether or not we are genuinely listening with the heart. There is a willingness on the part of a Christian to allow God to do with him whatever he wills. 'You are the block', writes Abbot Chapman, 'God is the sculptor; you cannot know what he is hitting you for, and you *never will* in this life'. And this is the equivalent of what is sometimes termed 'abandonment to divine providence'.

In connexion with this we do well to remember St Bernard's remark that it was not Christ's death that pleased the Father so much as his willingness to die.

Such willingness on the part of Christ was foreshadowed long before in the behaviour of Abraham; a person described in the Roman Missal as 'our father in faith'. His willingness was shown in his readiness to obey the promptings of God and leave his homeland and in his readiness to be tested even to the extent of being prepared to sacrifice his son Isaac (Gen 12: 23). And it is precisely this kind of loving readiness that we have to show in our commitment to God. Moreover whatever the cost may appear, the closer we attain to listening to God and attuning our wills to his, so we become truly free to love both responsibly and authentically. This is what Catherine of Siena was hinting at when she said that it was not nails that held Christ to the cross but love. It is this type of love which I tried to describe in chapter one.

A third indication that we are genuinely listening with the heart is the experience of participating in an intimate and reciprocal relationship with a Person. For the Christian it might be the Person of God the Father, Christ or the Holy Spirit. And since God is both transcendent and not subject to our limitations as well as being immanent or present there in our depths, an awareness of our own utter creatureliness and need of his support impels us to 'surrender' to him. It is from the strength of this personal relationship, (often thereby verifying Jesus' words: 'If anyone loves me he will keep my word, and my Father will love him, and we shall come to him and make our home with him' Jn 14:23), that a Christian should obtain the driving force to endure calmly the trials and tribulations associated with being one of God's poor or an 'anawim'.

It is then that the Christian also understands with more than his intellect what it means to be an adopted son of God and a brother of Christ. As St Paul was able to tell the Romans:

> Everyone moved by the Spirit is a son of God ... and it makes us cry out, 'Abba, Father!' The Spirit himself and our spirit bear witness that we are children of God. And if we are children we are heirs as well: heirs of God and coheirs with Christ, sharing his sufferings so as to share his glory.

Intuitively then the Christians will also appreciate the poet Blake's words, 'I am not a God afar off, I am a brother and friend; within your bosoms I reside, and you reside in me' *(Jerusalem)*.

This is clear from a fourth sign that such a person's experience is authentic. It is from an interior silence that the Christian receives an access of joy, vigour and strength — all gifts of the Holy Spirit. He understands with more than his mind what Deutero-Isaiah meant when he put this in the language of metaphor:

> He gives strength to the wearied,
> he strengthens the powerless ...
> Those who hope in God renew their strength,
> they put out wings like eagles.
> They run and do not grow weary,
> walk and never tire. (Is 40:29-31)

The need for renewal
Nevertheless the attainment of this condition, of what is actual and real and contrary to our own surface impressions so often, is rarely a once and for all experience, since we are all liable to regress. It is something requiring not merely vigilance but constant renewal. And on those occasions when we find it well nigh impossible to listen

in silence and attempt to communicate instead in more formal ways, we can still rest confident of God's concern: The Spirit too comes to help us in our weakness. For when we cannot choose words in order to pray properly, the Spirit himself expresses our plea in a way that could never be put into words . . . (Rom 8:26). So long indeed that we are on earth the tension of living the Christian life and dwelling at peace with the different but related parts of our make up will remain.

Listening with the heart then means not only cultivating inner peace, co-operating with the will of God, experiencing a personal relationship with God, receiving an access of joy, vigour and strength, but also being moved by the Holy Spirit. Without the help of the Holy Spirit Christians are liable to act in vain. Indeed, whenever we endeavour to help others without previously having listened to God first, it is likely that we shall do them more harm than good. We shall be relying merely on our own unguided efforts and risk projecting on them our own ideas, obsessions, ambitions and desires.

If however we do seek to encounter God in silence and in the ground of our being, our prayer will not merely permeate every area of our lives, bring inner peace and endow our lives with meaning and strength, but it will create a thirst for God in those around us. When most fruitful, action and certainly contemplative prayer are closely connected. This has been admirably put by Thomas Merton:

> Action and contemplation now grow together into one life and one unity. They become two aspects of the same thing. Action is charity looking outward to other men, and contemplation is charity drawn to its own divine source. Action is the stream and con-

templation is the spring. The spring remains more important than the stream, for the only thing that really matters is for love to spring up inexhaustibly from the infinite abyss of Christ and God *(No Man Is An Island)*.

The value of listening with the heart
Generally speaking, when we consider God either in conversation or study, we employ terms which attempt to describe him or give us information about him. Similarly, when we listen to music or poetry, or are moved by art, singing or dancing (especially when incorporated into worship) our emotions are capable of being uplifted to God. In the first instance our minds are utilized and in the second our feelings. Neither of them should be despised or underestimated; they are the tools of practical everyday living and were created by God.

But when we seek to relate to God in silence and in our souls at their deepest centre, we penetrate beyond the region of both intellect and emotion. It is there and in proportion to the extent that we allow ourselves to surrender entirely as it were with purity of intent into God's possession that he may respond. This is the meaning of listening with the heart; the silent but utterly attentive waiting on God.

Should anyone doubt the need for listening with the heart even in our relations with others, or what Martin Buber has termed 'being there in spirit', it is sobering to read his account of a time when he admits to not having done so:

> One afternoon I had a visit from an unknown man, without being there in spirit. I certainly did not fail to let the meeting be friendly, I did not treat him any

more remissly than all his contemporaries who were in the habit of seeking me out ... I conversed attentively and openly with him — only I omitted to guess the questions which he did not put. Later ... I learned ... that he had come to me not casually ... not for a chat but for a decision *(Between Man and Man)*.

The consequence, according to Buber himself, of his not 'being there in spirit' and failing to meet genuinely the man behind the talk between them, was that the man had left and subsequently committed suicide.

If that is what can occur only too easily between one person and another, what must be the consequences for the Christian who fails to listen with his heart to God?

8
God's activity in history: the foundation of prayer

The good news
Unless a Christian listens with his heart and cultivates all the qualities that such listening entails, he is liable to pursue dead ends for the greater part of his life. Perhaps that is fundamentally why so many Christians are disillusioned, frustrated or simply dissatisfied today. It is too easy to fail to acknowledge that until we become progressively more self-forgetful neither our love of God nor of our neighbour can increase in strength and depth.

Equally however it is just as easy to become concerned simply with our own individual perfection instead of attempting to play our part within the whole people of God. What we need therefore to avoid the cultivation of individual piety alone is to understand clearly the purpose of the Church of which all baptized Christians in differing degrees are members.

A great danger today among Christians is their proneness to adopting a new type of triumphalism in place of the old. This new type regards the Church as existing essentially to lead the vanguard of social change in society. But is this its primary function? Whilst never denying that Christians who make up the Church have a heavy duty to be concerned with the betterment of whatever society they may be living in (especially those in the Third World) and to pay more than lip service to causes of justice and peace, shouldn't they first see how they regard the Word of God that is both Christ himself and the good news he brings?

It was a religious message that Jesus brought into the world, of which its moral and social implications form only a part. To study the Christian message through political, economic or even moral spectacles alone is misguided. Such studies are not faithful to Jesus' message in its entirety.

More than ever today what is required is for us to understand Jesus and the Gospel he preached in terms of a gift from God to which the Christian should respond with praise and gratitude. The Church's primary function is therefore one of celebration in word and sacrament. And celebration inevitably carries with it connotations of joy.

Revelation

At this point, when attempting to discover why the Church should comprise a people of joy, it is impossible to avoid the technical term 'revelation'. In ordinary usage the word means that which is unveiled or disclosed. For the Christian it is the term he employs to describe his belief that God has freely chosen to show us what lies beyond the normal reach of human inquiry about himself. Revelation also includes the action by which God emerged from his obscurity, called to man, and invited him to enter into a loving relationship with him. A Christian's faith is his response to revelation. Knowing his own creatureliness and need of being rescued from his weak, selfish and proud tendencies, how could a Christian (at least one acquainted with God in his depths) fail but to be joyful when he considers such love on the part of God?

According to Paul (Ephesians 1:9-10) God indeed had a plan for the rescue or salvation of man in mind from all eternity; a plan which would reach its climax at the coming into the world of his Son, Jesus. In other words this was both an 'unveiling' of himself and a method of reconciling fallen man with him. Such a notion necessarily implies the idea of an intervention in the affairs of man. It also includes the concept of an encounter between persons — God and man; one speaking and the other listening.

Instances of God addressing and encountering men in the Old Testament are manifold. God called Abraham for example and Moses conversed with God, especially on Sinai where the people of Israel formally entered into a covenant relationship with God. Succeeding prophets throughout the ages expressed what God had imprinted in their hearts and minds. But what did God say and indicate that he expected of man?

Threads in revelation
God first revealed himself as a living and personal being — 'He who Is' — and not a dumb idol. He also made it clear that he is master of the cosmos or Lord of the nations. This was made plain through the prophets. Amos cast light on God's justice. Hosea emphasized his tender and exclusive love. Isaiah showed his grandeur and transcendence. Jeremiah taught God's preference for an interior religion. Deutero-Isaiah revealed him to be a universal God.

Moreover the persistent thread running through the whole of revelation in the Old Testament is God's concern for the salvation of man; a rescue necessary ever since the time when man first deliberately turned his back on God in disobedience.

Salvation is most usually couched in covenant terms, especially since the events on Sinai. It was linked with deliverance from slavery in Egypt. It was extended into the idea of a kingdom and early on with David and his dynasty. Already in the Old Testament however there were indications that God would at some time enter into a new covenant. These signs were present in reference to God's lordship over all the nations, and in mention of a mysterious 'Son of Man' approaching on clouds of heaven, a Messiah emerging from the priestly line and a servant of Yahweh who would rescue man through suffering.

As we read the Old Testament these are some of the major themes that we have to bear in mind. We have to see it as the moulding and shaping of a people in readiness for the supreme revelation; a gradual unveiling and unfolding of a pattern present in the mind of God from all eternity.

If we do not detect such a plan we risk viewing the Old Testament as merely an ancient collection of fables, war stories and inexplicable happenings or else as occasional uplifting literature. And without the record of the Old Testament, how would a Christian understand the coming of Jesus Christ? How would he interpret the words of the author of the Letter to the Hebrews when he writes: 'God, who at sundry times and in divers manners spoke in past times to the fathers by the prophets, last of all in these days he has spoken to us by his Son' (Heb 1:1).

Doesn't a Christian who is endeavouring to listen with his heart and worship alongside the rest of the people of God need therefore to set aside time each day to study the scriptures in order to learn who it is he will encounter in the silence at his centre and in the liturgy of the Church? If he does not, then he risks greatly merely creating a void and finding only himself.

On the other hand, if the Christian has immersed himself in the ways of God in the Old Testament he will understand that revelation is essentially inter-personal, that it proceeds from the initiative of God, that sin can be understood as man refusing to listen to God's Word (in other words he hardens his heart), and that God's plan for man extends beyond his life here on earth.

Just as important if not more, such a Christian will be prepared to understand more deeply the unique self-revelation of God on the stage of human history — the coming to earth of God's Son in the shape of a man. He will be able to make his own the words of St Ignatius of Antioch when he says: 'In Jesus Christ, Incarnate Word, the Son is present in our midst. He speaks, preaches, testifies to what he has seen and heard in the bosom of his Father'.

As one would therefore expect, the New Testament is really volume two in the story of salvation. Whereas volume one begins with creation and the disobedience of man, volume two records how a second Adam came to the rescue. Volume two is therefore the crown and climax of Scripture. Continuity and resemblance persist throughout the two parts, but in the New Testament revelation becomes clearer; the process of 'unveiling' becomes of surpassing importance. It is small wonder then that St Jerome could say that 'Ignorance of Scripture is ignorance of Christ'. But what does the listening Christian learn from the New Testament about Jesus?

What the Bible tells us of Jesus
First he comes to appreciate that Jesus existed before the incarnation. This pre-existence was already foreshadowed in the Old Testament in the Book of Proverbs:

> God created me when his purpose first unfolded,
>   before the oldest of his works.
> From everlasting I was firmly set,
>   from the beginning, before earth came into being.
> (Prov 8:22-23)

When a Christian reads in John's gospel such things as the prologue — 'In the beginning was the Word: the Word was with God and the Word was God' — he is not therefore surprised.

Equally, when in the same gospel he finds Jesus describing himself as 'the bread of life' (Jn 6:35) he is reminded in the Book of Proverbs of Wisdom's invitation to 'Come and eat my bread, drink the wine I have prepared!' (Prov 9:5). In other words, all that was previously spoken of in reference to God's wisdom is now revealed to apply in fact to the person of Jesus:

> Wisdom is a breath of the power of God,
> pure emanation of the glory of the Almighty;
> hence nothing impure can find a way into her.
> She is a reflection of the eternal light,
> untarnished mirror of God's active power,
> image of his goodness. (Wis 7: 25-26)

This identification of Jesus with the Father is made explicit in the famous exchange between Jesus and his disciple Philip:

> Philip said, 'Lord, let us see the Father and then we shall be satisfied' . . . Jesus replied, 'To have seen me

is to have seen the Father, so how can you say Let us see the Father? Do you believe that I am in the Father and the Father is in me?' (Jn 14:8-10)

Knowing full well, however, that the Jews were anticipating the advent of a Messiah or anointed king and especially one who would rescue them politically from Roman rule, Jesus went out of his way to use instead the mysterious title 'Son of Man'. This would seem to be a combination of Isaiah's prophecy concerning the coming of a suffering Servant of Yahweh who would carry the sins of his people — 'a man of sorrow and familiar with suffering' (Is 53:3) — and of Daniel's telling of the 'coming on clouds of heaven one like a son of man' (Dan 7:13). Hence it is we read of the Last Judgment in Matthew as the time when 'The Son of Man comes in his glory escorted by all the angels, then he will take his seat on his throne of glory. All the nations will be assembled before him, and he will separate one from another as the shepherd separates sheep from goats' (Mt 25: 31-32).

It is clear then that though Jesus did not deny his divinity, he deliberately chose instead not the path of earthly glory but that of 'kenosis' — a technical expression meaning self-emptying. When his divinity was expressed it was done obliquely.

When one asks therefore how did Jesus differ from other scribes and teachers of religion of the time, it is necessary to look more closely than usual. Like them he taught in the synagogue, worshipped in the temple, paid his temple tax, gathered around him a circle of disciples, disputed along the same lines, coined proverbs and parables and was not opposed to almsgiving, prayer and fasting, so what was the difference? The only external differences were that he had women followers and was very familiar with publicans and sinners. The clue to Jesus' fundamental difference is that people 'were astonished at his teaching, for he taught them as one who had authority, and not as the scribes' (Mk 1:22). Whereas the usual scribe spoke as one learned in the scriptures, Jesus in addition clearly spoke from the intimacy of his relationship with his Father.

But there were several other astonishing features about his ministry. In the first place it occupied from two to four years only at the most, and yet he gave no evidence of being in a hurry. On his travels or in the company of his friends he deliberately spent many hours in solitary prayer. In himself he epitomised calmness; a quality evident at his trial.

Then, although his listeners were used to being taught in parables, those of Jesus were of a kind in which God was found everywhere. Whether he was talking of birds, water, grapes, lost sheep, the thief in the night, children, harlots, farmers, priests or merchants, they were all part of the vehicle he employed to illustrate the transparency of this world and how the visible indicated the existence of invisible realities.

In his work Jesus also acted with absolute confidence. To a sick man he would simply say: 'take up your pallet and go home'; to an unclean spirit he would issue the command 'be quiet and come out'. And yet there was never aloofness from the affairs around him. He was very much involved in what was taking place wherever he happened to be. Even his indignation (such as when the disciples wanted to keep children away from him), his intolerance (as when the disciples were envious of each other) and his anger (as when James and John wanted to punish the inhospitable Samaritans) were evidence of a very great love. Jesus became most furious when his friends let themselves down.

In the same way that one has to seek more deeply to discover Jesus' difference from other religious teachers, so it is necessary to search as it were beneath the surface of the New Testament to find signs that Jesus was aware of his divinity. This is rendered harder by the fact that he himself expressed it obliquely, but the indications are not lacking.

No ordinary Jew would have dared to address God the Father, even in intimate prayer, as 'Abba'. And yet that was what Jesus did and encouraged his disciples to do the same. Moreover when Jesus spoke of how if this temple (his body) were to be destroyed it would be raised again in three days, was he not obviously referring to the Resurrection? Similarly, when he promised to supply the people with eternal food (his body and blood) do we not have another indication of his awareness of his divine mission? From his references to himself at different times as the vine and his Father as the vine-dresser, as the light of the world, as the gate of the sheepfold and as the way, the truth and the life, can we remain in doubt?

Consequences
It follows therefore that if we accept Jesus' claims, together with the continued existence of the Church as the primary evidence for the Resurrection, then we have little choice but to follow the path that he laid down for his disciples.

> And Jesus called them (his disciples) to him and said to them, 'You know that those who are supposed to rule over the Gentiles lord it over them, and their

great men exercise authority over them. But it shall not be so among you; but whoever would be great among you must be your servant, and whoever would be first among you must be slave of all' (Mk 10:42-44).

Clearly it is Jesus as Son of Man who came not to be served but to serve and give his life as a ransom for many (Mk 10:45) that Christians are called upon to emulate. Kenosis or self-emptying is the vocation of all of us. All that we previously discussed about love, service, sacrifice, suffering and the function of the People of God is now confirmed in scripture. Moreover the God who reveals this to us there is the same and identical with the God whom we encounter in personal prayer. Again therefore we are reminded that our rôle is to be the poor of God or the 'anawim' of the present day. But why should these be matters of celebration and joy?

Essentially and as a result of the new covenant instituted between God and man by Jesus at the Last Supper we now know that we have been rescued or saved. Moreover we are able to encounter Christ now in the sacraments, in our daily meditation on the Word as found in the Scriptures, in the liturgy of the Church, in the love of our fellow men and in the silence when we listen with our hearts. Not merely is our growth as human beings hereby assured but our freedom from loneliness has been guaranteed by Jesus himself:

> If you love me you will keep my commandments.
> I shall ask the Father
> and he will give you another Advocate
> to be with you for ever,
> that Spirit of truth
> whom the world can never receive

since it neither sees nor knows him;
but you know him,
because he is with you, he is in you.
I will not leave you orphans;
I will come back to you (Jn 14:15-18).

According to Jesus, this same counsellor or protector will teach us everything and remind us of all that he said (Jn 14:26). The same Spirit will lead us to the complete truth and tell us of the things to come (Jn 16:13). And according to Paul: 'What the Spirit brings is ... love, joy, peace, patience, kindness, goodness, trustfulness, gentleness and self-control' (Gal 5:22).

Instead then of a Christian being confused, depressed or even anxious, shouldn't he rather be making the words of Paul to the Ephesians his own?

Blessed be God the Father of our Lord Jesus Christ ... Before the world was made, he chose us, chose us in Christ, to be holy and spotless, and to live through love in his presence, determining that we should become his adopted sons, through Jesus Christ ... in whom, through his blood, we gain our freedom, the forgiveness of our sins ... He has let us know the mystery of his purpose, the hidden plan he so kindly made in Christ from the beginning.

The reality
But lest this be considered remote from the experience of everyday life as known to the Christian in present-day society, it might be helpful to consider what happened not so long ago to a priest called to the bedside of a man dying in hospital.

When the priest arrived at the hospital he was shocked

to find the dying man was more or less his own age. The physical difference between them however was startling. The man in the bed was bent doubled through finding it difficult to breathe, especially as he only had one lung. In addition he was riddled with cancer. It was a matter of minutes before he was to die.

The priest asked him to nod if he understood that his visitor was a priest, and he did so. He then asked him to nod if he understood that he was about to anoint him, and again the man did so. Finally — even though the man was soon to slip away — the priest asked him to nod if he understood and wanted to receive Holy Communion. This time the nod was unmistakable. And so the dying man was anointed and given the Sacrament. What was astonishing was that, though the man could not speak and was obviously suffering dreadful pain, after he had received Holy Communion — and knew that he had — he became calmer and obviously more at ease. He died a few minutes later with the priest still by the bedside.

Before leaving the ward the priest asked the sister in charge if the man's relatives had been informed. He wondered why they had not been present. To his amazement the priest learnt that the man had no relatives. He had been an orphan since childhood and had spent the whole of his earthly life in institutions and hostels. There was no one in the world who would mourn his death.

On the other hand, he had himself fully understood what it was to be an adopted son of God. He had indicated that he fully knew that Jesus is the Bread of Life. And at the end of his life here on earth, there was no doubting the reality of the peace in his heart; a peace which passed all understanding and which is usually associated with the poor of God.

The dimension which the dying man had been unable to experience, except only theoretically, was what might be termed the communal aspect of his religion. Fortunately more and more Christians today are becoming aware of this dimension. And lest it be considered that what has so far been said about prayer applies essentially only to the individual Christian, it would seem important to close with a chapter illustrating how all that has so far been written might equally well and profitably be pursued in a group context. Prayer in groups is a very real antidote to the notion that man is an island.

9
Prayer in groups: charismatic prayer

Preliminaries
More and more, in parishes up and down the country, Christians are gathering together not simply to discuss the meaning and relevance of their faith to the modern world but to pray. For those unacquainted with group prayer or attending for the first time, such gatherings are sometimes a source of embarrassment. But in fact should they be? Didn't Jesus say: 'Where two or three are gathered together in my name, there am I in the midst of them'? Provided then a Christian is prepared to attend a prayer group without preconceptions and prejudices, it is often a source of wonderment to such a person why he was either reluctant or fearful to do so in the first place.

If a group of Christians meet together with the deliberate intention of praying, at least for the first few sessions it might be useful if beforehand everyone has studied a particular text from Scripture. The value of this is that it gives members a sense of assurance, acts as an anchor sheet and gives each person something to come prepared with to the meeting.

Once the group has assembled, its leader (possibly this rôle is filled on a revolving basis according to whose house the group meets in) would open the proceedings by offering his or her thoughts on the text agreed upon earlier. One by one the leader could then elicit from each person present his views on the matter.

It would seem important to stress that the idea behind this is to provide a solid basis for the prayer that is to follow. The exploration of the chosen text needs to be done with this in mind; it should not be regarded as an exercise in biblical exegesis but rather one of each individual attempting to determine how the words from Scripture apply to his or her daily life and relationships. 'What has this particular piece of Scripture to do with me?' 'What is this text asking of this group?' These are the sort of questions that should be being asked.

Provided such exploration is done gently and calmly and not used as a device for display of knowledge, the group might then equally deliberately foster an atmosphere of quiet and peace. This might be achieved by the group quietly singing a hymn, the contents of which would be along the same lines as the scriptural text. Alternatively a piece of music might be played or one person recite a piece of poetry which would gather up in a coherent whole the ideas previously put out by the group. Stillness and peace, however, are what the assembled group are attempting to attain. And unless particular members of the group are specifically gifted in the fields of music and mime, drama or poetry, it is often better that people remain still.

Another essential element is that participants should be gathered together clearly as a group. In other words they should be so seated or standing that each can hear with ease whatever any individual has to contribute and everything be done that is possible for the people present to be able to develop a group consciousness.

Above all, whatever position a person may choose, it should be that which enables the group to concentrate, to listen, to eliminate fidgeting and yet be utterly relaxed.

Group prayer
It is usual and often most natural for one's first spontaneous prayers after the preliminaries are over to be ones of thanksgiving and praise. Thanks may be offered by different members for life itself, the faith, the beauty of creation, love from God and one's family and friends, talents and opportunities for doing good and so on. These may be followed by prayers for forgiveness and acknowledgment of our failure to cultivate the presence of God at every moment of our day, of our failings in charity to others and of our own weakness in not realising our own potential with the help of God. Petitions either for specific things, occasions or persons are a third type which spring naturally to one's lips.

Nevertheless, though all these three kinds of prayer (and more) may occur within the group, they are still in a sense preparatory to the group's encounter with God in which the chief object is to listen with the heart.

Moreover, from all that has been said earlier it should be obvious that listening in this context is basically meeting with God. The nature of such a meeting eludes description since it is not comparable to many of our usual experiences, except those of being in the company of ones we love and with whom communication is at a deeper level than words.

Since we are human however and furthermore each unique, when such a meeting occurs different members of the group may respond in different ways. Some may be caught up into further spontaneous prayer, uttered in tongues. Others may seemingly withdraw into deep interior peace. The more regularly the group meets however and as its members increasingly become more open to God and each other, the tendency during encounters with God is for a pattern to emerge; a pattern of utterly simple prayers intervening with natural pauses and total silence.

The need for discernment

During the actual prayer sessions it is the responsibility of the group leader to exercise as fully as possible the art of discernment in order to eliminate all elements of possible hysteria, pretence and extreme emotionalism. In this connexion it is valuable to consider Simon Tugwell's words:

> The chief thing to be watched in prayer meetings is 'short circuiting'. It is all too easy to say 'Praise God!' at the top of your voice, just because everyone else is doing so. It is easy to pick up an external idiom of prayer without really entering into prayer. It is especially easy to get carried away quite unprofitably and unprofoundly by exuberant group singing. Singing is terribly important, but it must be prayer, not an evasion or a substitute for prayer.
>
> We should learn a deep interior silence, so that anything we say, or sing, or shout, comes from deep down . . .
>
> If we find ourselves praying in an assumed or unnatural voice (it can happen) we should beware. If we find ourselves thinking, 'Why isn't anything happening? I must try and stir things up!' we should beware. One thing we can be quite sure of: anything that is not fully *our* prayer, will not be God's prayer either. *(Did You Receive the Spirit?)*

Such discernment is particularly necessary if one attends prayer groups associated with the charismatic renewal.

Charismatic prayer
The charismatic renewal is probably most typified in its small local prayer groups where one encounters individuals from every kind of economic, social and educational background. More than a few in such gatherings were previously nominal rather than committed Christians; some have experienced private tragedies or deprivation in their lives. Most will testify to the change in their outlook, life-style and attitude to the Christian faith as a result of becoming involved in the renewal.

Not only are they reputed to take the Gospel and the sacraments more seriously, but most would claim to have experienced within themselves a 'release of the Holy Spirit'. This in its turn is said to have brought a more personal awareness of Jesus as Lord and a deepening of their commitment to him through shared and spontaneous prayer, as well as the bestowal of many gifts of the Holy Spirit.

Not all Christians have greeted the charismatic renewal with an uncritical eye. Some sincerely fear that it breeds élitism and excessive emotionalism, places too much emphasis on the experience known in traditional pentecostal terms as 'baptism in the Holy Spirit', gives too much prominence to 'extraordinary gifts' such as speaking in tongues, prophecy and healing, and is capable of alienating Christians dubbed as non-charismatics.

Certainly what seems to have escaped the notice of many involved in the charismatic renewal is that such experiences are not new in the life and history of the Church. What is possibly new is the discovery of a more widely appealing and communal (some would say populist) vehicle for conveying traditional ideas.

Throughout the ages spiritual writers have often referred to the need for a second conversion, as distinct from the sacraments of initiation, for those who have fallen into a state of tepidity. In classical terms this second conversion described in the writings of, for example, Henry Suso, Tauler, Catherine of Siena, Teresa of Avila and John of the Cross, is marked by a passive purgation of the senses which leads to what is known as the illuminative way. But even this is not considered enough for, according to John of the Cross, even if the senses of those who have entered on the illuminative way have to a great extent been purged of inertia, jealousy, impatience, dependence on spiritual feelings and so on, 'stains of the old man', which are like rust, remain. Hence he says, all this shows the need for the 'strong lye', that passive purgation of the spirit, that further conversion which marks the entrance to the perfect way known as the unitive.

When St John speaks of the three ways, purgative, illuminative and unitive, he is following closely the traditions of the Fathers, of Clement of Alexandria, Cassian, Augustine, Dionysius the Pseudo-Areopagite and the great teachers of the Middle Ages: Anselm, Hugh of St Victor, Albert the Great, Bonaventure and Thomas Aquinas. Moreover, the processes of the purgation of the senses and the spirit have been the subject of considerable scrutiny and documentation over the ages; they have been tested in time.

The three ways
The first is characterized by a prolonged aridity or 'dryness' and deprivation of the feelings in which an individual may have become complacent. Nevertheless,

if an intense desire for God and fear of offending him remains, this is taken as a sign that the purgation is of divine origin. In addition if an inclination towards prayer of simple regard, quiet and love, as opposed to other kinds, accompanies this state, this is regarded as further evidence that the second conversion is taking place. And provided the person perseveres through this crisis he is richly rewarded.

To employ the language of Dionysius and Thomas Aquinas, the soul then rises in a spiral movement from the mystery of the Incarnation to those of Christ's Passion, Resurrection, Ascension and Glory, then contemplates in these mysteries the radiance of the sovereign goodness of God; the soul simultaneously receives an abundance of light through the gift of understanding and a greater facility in prayer and an increase in apostolic fervour.

Even so, it is possible for those now on the illuminative way to regard these gifts possessively, to become unconsciously proud of their greater facility in prayer and apostolic work. In their search for God they may have found only themselves. Thus there is the need for a third conversion.

When this occurs, as described in *The Dark Night* of St John of the Cross, the person is deprived not only of spiritual feelings or consolations but also of supernatural lights on the mysteries of salvation, his ardent desires and ease in handling spiritual matters altogether. An individual also often experiences suffering in the shape of failure, ingratitude and calumnies.

This purgation of the spirit is the equivalent of the death of the old man in St Paul: 'Our old man is crucified with Jesus Christ, that the body of sin may be destroyed' (Rom 6:6). But if with courage and vigilance it results in perfect abandonment, then those who persist through this third conversion come to know God continuously. They contemplate the divine goodness in itself.

In the terminology again of both Dionysius and Thomas Aquinas, it is a movement of contemplation no longer straight or spiral but circular, like the flight of the eagle, which after rising to a great height, circles round and round, and hovers to view the horizon. One has entered on the unitive way.

The need for guidance and direction
Since conversion has played such a large part in the thought and teaching of the classical spiritual writers, it might seem appropriate to ask why it seems to have made so little impact on people in general. Could it be that their teaching was considered too individualistic and difficult of attainment for the majority? And could it be that the charismatic renewal is employing methods of conveying traditional ideas in simpler terms and in a manner more suited to contemporary man? How much does it owe to its communal dimension?

No Christian schooled in traditional spirituality could take exception to or be surprised by many of the experiences described by those in the charismatic renewal. We have probably all witnessed at least the therapeutic, healing and awakening effects that the renewal has had on individuals and groups. Even so, in traditional spirituality one always needed careful guidance and direction in attempting to pass through the processes of second and third conversions. Those involved in the charismatic renewal, who are attempting to reach the same goals, albeit by different routes, might do well therefore to heed at least the counsel of systematic theologians and biblical scholars. Only thus will the renewal become imbedded in mainstream Christianity.

The theologian F.A. Sullivan who is himself involved in the renewal recently had some firm advice to offer his brethren. Writing in *The Holy Spirit and Power* he remarked:

> The way people in the charismatic renewal are using the term 'charismatic' can very easily alienate the rest of the people of God who find themselves described as 'non-charismatics' ... The dangers of alienation become the more acute when a pastor learns that a group of his parishioners who speak of themselves as 'charismatics' are rejoicing that they have finally found a 'charismatic priest' to lead them in 'charismatic liturgy' and offer them 'charismatic ministry'.

As he goes on to point out, the question at issue is a basic one for the Church, namely what is a charism?

Instead of limiting our definition of a charism to such things as tongues, prophecy, healing and the like, it would seem vital to hold fast to a broader concept. And if a charism could be held to include *any* gift which contributes to the upbuilding and extension of the Christian community, many fears and suspicions might be allayed.

In the meantime, to avoid the dangers of élitism, excessive emotionalism, biblical fundamentalism and of attaching too much importance to 'extraordinary' charisms, those involved in the charismatic renewal could do worse than both study the classical writers mentioned earlier and cultivate the art of listening with the heart.

Conclusion
The acid test of the genuineness of both individual and group prayer will always be the fruit they bear in the

lives of those who are attempting to relate with God and their neighbour. Any sincere encounter with God will inevitably leave a mark and this is particularly so if one perseveres in prayer, always taking Jesus at his word that anything we ask for in his name he will do it (Jn 14:14).

Our problem so often is not that we do not in theory see the value of deepening our prayer lives through deliberate cultivation of silence, interior peace and listening with the heart, but that in practice we are frightened. We are afraid of what an encounter with God might entail in the sense of being required to be 'open', to love and to become one of his poor. Secretly we might despise our own immaturity and failure to have developed an adult relationship with our Creator; we might bemoan our loneliness and pay lip service to Jesus' assurance that he would be with us always. And with our heads if not our hearts we may accept that God the Father did intervene in human history when he sent his Son into the world.

Such was the problem of the rich young man in the Gospel who enquired of Jesus what he must do to inherit eternal life. When Jesus heard that the man had kept all God's commandments from his earliest days, he told him: 'There is still one thing you lack. Sell all that you own and distribute the money to the poor, and you will have treasure in heaven; then come, follow me'. According to St Luke (18:23), the young man was filled with sadness when he heard this, for he was very rich.

Legend has it that, after going away sorrowfully and not finding satisfaction by himself, the rich young man did after all become one of Jesus' disciples, for in St Matthew's account Jesus had 'looked steadily at him and loved him'; something he never forgot. And the same can apply to all those who permit Jesus to do the same to them.

Further reading

(Anon) *The Cloud of Unknowing* (trans. Wolters)
Anthony Bloom, *Living Prayer; School for Prayer*
Ladislaus Boros, *Between God and Man*
Carlo Carretto, *Letters from the Desert; In Search of the Beyond*
Viktor Frankl, *The Doctor and the Soul*
Erich Fromm, *The Fear of Freedom*
Mark Gibbard, *Twentieth-Century Men of Prayer*
Dag Hammarskjöld, *Markings*
Michael Hollings, *Day by Day; I Will Be There*
C.S. Lewis, *Letters to Malcolm: Chiefly on Prayer*
Thomas Merton, *Seeds of Contemplation; Contemplative Prayer*
Simon Tugwell, *Did You Receive the Spirit?*
Michael Quoist, *Christ is Alive!*
Gerald Vann, *The Son's Course; The Divine Pity*
René Voillaume, *Seeds of the Desert; Brothers of Men*